Blacks Don't Bowl

Blacks Don't Bowl

Vadney S. Haynes

Playwrights Canada Press
Toronto • Canada

Playwrights Canada Press
The Canadian Drama Publisher
215 Spadina Avenue, Suite 230, Toronto, Ontario CANADA M5T 2C7
416-703-0013 fax 416-408-3402
orders@playwrightscanada.com • www.playwrightscanada.com

Financial support provided by the taxpayers of Canada and Ontario through the Canada Council for the Arts and the Department of Canadian Heritage through the Book Publishing Industry Development Programme, and the Ontario Arts Council.

Canada

The Canada Council for the Arts
Le Conseil des Arts du Canada

ONTARIO ARTS COUNCIL
CONSEIL DES ARTS DE L'ONTARIO

Front cover photos: Bowler © Phil Carpenter, Bowling Ball © 2006 Jupiterimages Corp.
Production Editor/Cover design: JLArt

Library and Archives Canada Cataloguing in Publication

Haynes, Vadney S., 1951-

Blacks don't bowl / Vadney S. Haynes.

A play.

ISBN 978-0-88754-466-8

1. Blacks--Canada--Drama. I. Title.

PS8615.A858B53 2007 C812'.6 C2007-900245-5

First edition: January 2007.
Printed and bound by Canadian Printco at Scarborough, Canada.

For Shelley and for Black people everywhere.

Playwright's Notes

The title of my play can be taken as a statement of fact, an explicit injunction, or an implicit question. Whatever one's take on the title, the play itself is intended to serve as a basis for dialogue not only between you and others, but also with yourself. To get Black people to examine some of the elements that make up what it means to be Black was the creative impulse behind my writing the play. Identity defines, but it also confines. Separating one from the other is not always easy – and it's impossible unless there is a willingness to question that which is taken as a given. I hope my play provides one such opportunity.

They say it takes a village to raise a child. It also takes a community to mount a play. In the course of writing (and re-writing) *Blacks Don't Bowl*, I've been priviledged in having the help of many people towards the realization of what's on stage. I'd like to offer my deepest thanks to the following: the many actors who took part in workshops and public readings both here in Montreal and in Toronto; Teesri Duniya Theatre where formal work on shaping the play began; AfriCanadian Playwrights Festival; Toronto's Factory Theatre and its CrossCurrents Festival; Kate Bligh (thanks for your patience); Bill Lane and Alison Sealy-Smith. A special thank you to former Black Theatre Workshop Artistic Director Rachael Van Fossen for getting the whole thing started; current Black Theatre Workshop Artistic Director Tyrone Benskin; Nigel Shawn Williams, not only for his great direction of the play, but also for pointing me, script-wise, in the right direction; the wonderful actors who've made me proud for having written the play in the first place; and to Shelley Tepperman for her dramaturgical wisdom and deep support.

Blacks Don't Bowl was first produced by Black Theatre Workshop at the MAI (Montréal, Arts Interculturels) in March 2006 with the following company:

Quincy Armorer	Maurice
Tamara Brown	Janeen
Jesse Aaron Dwyre	Sherman
Matthew Kabwe	Frank
Omari Newton	Pinto
Elizabeth Robertson	Johanne

Directed by Nigel Shawn Williams
Dramaturg: Shelley Tepperman
Set/Lighting Designer: Ana Cappelluto
Costume Designer: Sarah Hall
Technical Director: Steve Schön
Sound Designer: Troy Slocum
Stage mananger: Todd Bricker
Assistant Director: Edouard Fontaine
Assistant Designer: Catharine Boivin
Apprentice Stage Manager: Lori Allen

• • •

Characters

FRANK, A professional in his mid-forties.

PINTO, A student in his early twenties.

JANEEN, A photographer in her late twenties.

MAURICE, A visual artist in his early thirties.

JOHANNE, An arts administrator in her late thirties.

SHERMAN, A part-time student in his early twenties.

Blacks Don't Bowl

ACT I

1st FRAME — THE ART CRITIC

Thursday evening. End of August. Outside an art gallery. We hear FRANK before we see him backing out of the building.

FRANK You goddamn artists. Don't artists think? If you did you would see that this is dangerous. Where's your sense of responsibility? Black Reflections? Black Reflections? What sick mirrors have you been looking in? *(pause)* No. There is no room for other voices. There's only the voice that says this is wrong, wrong, and does not belong in a public gallery. I'm going to make certain of that. When you came to me asking for support, if I'd known it was for this garbage I'd've thrown you out right there and then. I should have asked more questions. My mistake. You took advantage of my good nature. Your mistake. Now I'm going to do the only responsible thing. I'm going to shut you down.

Lights out. Lights up on the Funny Bones Comedy Club.

PINTO Good evening and welcome to the Funny Bones Comedy Club. I went for an interview last week for a government job. During the interview they asked me what efficiency meant to me. I said that it was the ability to do the most important things in the least amount of time, leaving plenty of time to do the least important things. I'm on the shortlist.

You've heard that the government wants to hire more visible minorities for the civil service but says it's having a hard time finding any. Really? Can you imagine not being able to find me? I mean you saw at least one visible minority today didn't you? On your way home tonight, if you see another one, would you be so kind as to tell them that the government is looking for them so that they can give them a job.

I recently felt that it was time I exposed myself to a little culture, broaden my horizons, so I decided to visit some art galleries. At one of the galleries, in one of the rooms, there was an installation consisting of 50 pairs of identical athletic socks hanging on a clothesline. That's all there was in the room. I thought I'd walked into the laundry room by mistake, but no, it was part of the show and it had a title: "The Agony of Representation." So I stood there for a while staring at it figuring a woman would walk in, think I'm a sensitive, post-modern male and take me home. That didn't happen, so I tried to understand what it meant. As I stood there, it came to me in a flash that what it meant was that I should have been somewhere else doing something that had meaning. So I went home, did my laundry, folded it all very nicely, put the pile on my front stairs with a little sign that said: "The Ecstasy of Sanitation." It sold.

Lights out.

2nd FRAME — OBVIOUSLY OBLIVIOUS

Later that Thursday evening. Inside the art gallery.

JANEEN A memorable day.

MAURICE All the way 'round.

JANEEN I'm sorry I ever suggested inviting that horrible man.

MAURICE Did you see the vein in the middle of his forehead pop up?

JANEEN I know. I thought he was going to stroke out.

MAURICE I'd heard he could be difficult, but nothing like that.

JANEEN He can't spoil our accomplishment. Pour me some more Mo'.

MAURICE Baby, you and me, what a team. Nobody's doing the kind of work we are, and that's because nobody's saying what we're saying. Especially Black artists.

JANEEN Remember what I said at the restaurant last—

MAURICE Politicians have agendas. I don't. Artists just need three things: a vision, the talent to realize that vision, and the balls to defend it. Everything else is a distraction. Nothing or no one should get in the way.

JANEEN Nothing?

MAURICE Nothing.

JANEEN You're forgetting the responsibility that goes with all that. The responsibility to bring those who don't see what you see along with you. That's part of being an artist.

MAURICE My responsibility is to present what I believe is the truth. That's all being an artist is.

She pours them some champagne and flips through a film program.

JANEEN Hey, "À Bout de souffle" is playing at Cité Rep. I love that film. Jean Seberg never knew what hit her, she was just swept off her feet by Belmondo.

MAURICE jumps up, picks JANEEN up and swooshes her around the room.

MAURICE Like that? Is that what women want?

JANEEN Only if they've taken some Gravol first. I promised my mother I'd help her pick up some things in the morning. You know I still can't figure out why she doesn't like driving by herself. I don't know what she's afraid of.

MAURICE Why does she have to be afraid of anything? Maybe she just doesn't like driving alone. I don't like wool socks, horror movies, tangerines. I don't like Van Gogh, scented candles, and I don't like postcards. What are you gonna make of that? Nothing. 'Cause there's nothing to be made. I just don't like them and that's that. *Point finale.*

JANEEN Okay Mr. Surface.

MAURICE Mr. Shiny Surface.

Lights out.

3rd FRAME — FUNDAMENTALLY DIVIDED

Friday morning. Montreal Black Association office, functionally furnished, containing posters of Caribbean tourist scenes and famous Black people such as Rosa Parks, Frederick Douglas, Martin Luther King Jr., Maya Angelou. FRANK is punching up a phone number. Lights up on JOHANNE Tétreault in her office as she answers the telephone.

JOHANNE Johanne Tétreault *à la appareil.*

FRANK This is Frank Simmons, Executive Director of the Montreal Black Association.

JOHANNE *Bonjour.*

FRANK Have you seen it?

JOHANNE *Pardon*?

FRANK Have you seen it?

JOHANNE I don't know. Could you tell me what you're speaking about Monsieur Simmons.

FRANK That goddamn art show you allowed to happen. Black Reflections.

JOHANNE Oh yes, Reflets Noirs. Very interes—

FRANK Did you see it before it opened?

JOHANNE Yes, sort of.

FRANK Sort of? Sort of? What does that mean?

JOHANNE As part of the application package there were some photos and video clips included.

FRANK You obviously didn't see anything wrong with them.

JOHANNE No, I'm sorry, I'm afraid not. And why are—?

FRANK Were there any Black people involved in the decision about the funding?

JOHANNE No.

FRANK Pull your support from the show, close it and make a public statement saying that the Conseil des Arts Métropolitain does not support anything which is offensive and damaging to the Black community. I want a press release tomorrow saying exactly that.

JOHANNE I don't understand what—

FRANK It's simple. Close the show.

JOHANNE Close the show.

FRANK Now you got it.

JOHANNE That's not possible, but I want to hear—

FRANK Yes it is and you'll hear all right.

JOHANNE Please tell me, Monsieur Simmons. I'm listening to you.

FRANK That so-called art show is an insult and it's upsetting.

JOHANNE I can hear that you're very upset.

FRANK Damn right I am. Who wouldn't be. I mean what self-respecting Black person wouldn't be. Those pictures, those images, are an affront to everything that we—my organization—has been struggling to counter for so long. You turn around and find out that behind your back there are others fighting to undo your accomplishments.

JOHANNE I can't believe the artists would be trying to do anything like that. Perhaps you misunderstood their inten—

FRANK No I did not. There's no mistaking what I saw, and I don't care what their intention was, but I do care what the effect is and that's why something has to be done, and I want you to do it.

JOHANNE What you're suggesting—

FRANK It's a demand: a demand I'm making on behalf of the Black community.

JOHANNE I will do my best to see how I can help you. If you would like, I will see if I can arrange a meeting for you with the artists.

FRANK I don't want a meeting. I don't want to talk with those damn fools. When they came to see me they tricked me. They made it all sound so innocent.

Lights down on JOHANNE. Lights up on the Montreal Black Association office. Two months earlier. PINTO and FRANK are working on files, the computer, writing notes etc.

Make sure everything's properly labelled. When I tell you that this is big and important it's because it's big and important.

PINTO Okay.

FRANK One year. One whole year of pulling this thing together and now the last few details. Finally, it's going to happen. The Black Community Forum. Why are you making that silly face?

PINTO It's my doubting face. Do you want to see my silly face?

FRANK Get rid of it because that's one of the reasons this is being done. Too many doubting Thomases. "It can't be done," "Forget it, don't waste your time," "You can't bring the Black community together, it exists just in name." I'm sick and tired of hearing all of that. You, you're too young to be so cynical.

PINTO I'm not being cynical.

FRANK Yes you are. Is that what they're teaching you in Political Science these days? You want a lesson in politics, do this job for a little while.

PINTO When do you want the notices to go out?

FRANK I told you already. This Thursday.

PINTO No, you didn't.

FRANK Yes I did. Don't be difficult. Want some of this sandwich?

PINTO No thanks.

FRANK You're sure?

PINTO Very sure.

FRANK Doesn't sound that way to me.

PINTO Does to me.

FRANK I think you're just being difficult.

PINTO It's not in my nature.

FRANK That's nonsense. Everybody has it in them to be difficult.

PINTO You would know.

FRANK What? Of course at the Forum there's going to be all sorts of quarrelling, and bickering, the usual nonsense.

PINTO Then why are you doing it?

FRANK I repeat: what are they teaching you in that university? It's about the process. Getting the Black people in this city to see that they have an opportunity, no, a responsibility to speak out about the things that affect their lives. Words lead to actions.

Go over there.

PINTO Over—?

FRANK —there.

Okay, now read out loud the vision statement of the Montreal Black Association.

PINTO Out loud? Okay, okay.

"The Montreal Black Association seeks to promote at all times and in all ways the values of responsibility, empowerment and pride so that the hopes, aspirations and needs of the Black community can be realized."

FRANK I wrote it myself.

PINTO Really?

FRANK Think you're funny?

PINTO You saw the message I left you?

FRANK reads a note.

FRANK That man misses more meetings than he attends. He should resign from the Executive if he can't fulfill his duties.

PINTO Maybe he leads a double life as a secret agent for the Israeli Secret Service.

FRANK Don't be stupid, he's Black.

PINTO And…?

FRANK It's Israel. They're Jews. The Israeli Secret Service doesn't have Black spies.

PINTO Exactly. Perfect cover.

FRANK You talk nonsense. What an imagination.

PINTO Gets me through my courses.

FRANK Listen Pinto, I'd like to thank you for the good work you've done here as our summer intern, so I'm inviting you to come for dinner when this is all over.

PINTO Thanks, maybe.

FRANK Plus you get to meet my wonderful wife and daughter. Aren't they something?

PINTO Yes they are. You're a very fortunate man.

FRANK Damn right I am. There's an empty place for you.

PINTO I'll think about it and let you know soon.

FRANK What's the problem?

PINTO No problem.

FRANK Good. And my niece from Ottawa is with us for the summer. You'd like her. She's very smart and attractive.

PINTO I'm sure she is.

FRANK Do you have a girlfriend?

PINTO Not really.

FRANK Not really. Either you do or you don't. Are you gay?

PINTO I was until I came in here this morning.

FRANK Think you're funny?

PINTO It's a little complicated Frank.

FRANK Then make it simple. It's settled. You come for dinner.

PINTO I—

FRANK Dorothy will be so pleased. I've told her about you.

PINTO I—

FRANK I'll call her and tell her that—

PINTO Frank.

FRANK Yes?

PINTO I—I—

There's a knock at the door.

FRANK Come on. Spit it out. I'm half listening.

PINTO It can wait, there's someone at the door.

FRANK I know. Come in.

MAURICE and JANEEN enter.

JANEEN We're looking for Frank Simmons.

FRANK That's me.

MAURICE Pleased to meet you. I'm Maurice Wilson.

JANEEN And I'm Janeen Danner. We spoke on the phone a couple of weeks ago.

FRANK We spoke? I don't remember any—

MAURICE You called him didn't you?

JANEEN Yes I did. And said we'd like to come by to talk to you about our art exhibition.

MAURICE Black Reflections/Reflets Noirs.

JANEEN Meeting you here today at 3:30.

FRANK I don't remember. Let me check. So what can I do for you?

MAURICE We're mounting a show at the end of August.

JANEEN A very important show.

MAURICE That documents certain elements of contemporary Black reality.

JANEEN A reality that says a lot about what it's like to be simultaneously valued and despised as a people.

MAURICE We think we've captured the response to that in our exhibition.

JANEEN The exhibit—

FRANK Whoa. Wait a minute.

JANEEN Oh, sorry. Going too fast?

FRANK No. Not fast enough. You haven't told me what it is you want from me.

MAURICE As Executive Director of the Montreal Black Association, we'd like it if—

JANEEN —we'd be honoured.

MAURICE We'd be honoured if you would say a few words at the vernissage to kick it off.

JANEEN We see what you and your organization are trying to do as very much in keeping with what we feel our work is trying to show.

MAURICE Perfect fit.

FRANK I don't know.

MAURICE It won't take much of your time. Five minutes. It could be an opportunity to—

FRANK I don't know if I'll have the time and I know nothing about art.

MAURICE But you know what you like.

FRANK No. Don't think I can even say that.

MAURICE Sure you do.

FRANK No I don't. It's just not a part of my world.

JANEEN But it is. Art is everywhere and in everything. People have been conditioned to think too narrowly. You're probably an artist and don't even know it.

FRANK No I'm not.

MAURICE There you go again. Just because someone paints a landscape, or makes a vase on their community centre pottery wheel does not make them an artist.

JANEEN What I'm talking about is the importance of perception and how that gives each person a unique, almost un-shareable understanding of the world that then serves as the filter for all experience. That is the basis of art. And when you take control of those perceptions and experiences, no one can tell you who or what you are.

FRANK I don't understand any of what you're talking about.

PINTO Yes you do. That's what you were saying before. The importance of getting the Black community to take responsibility for what happens to it. It's right up there on the wall. I'll go over there and read it out loud.

FRANK Not necessary. What is it you do exactly?

MAURICE I'm a videographer and a visual artist.

JANEEN And I'm a photographer.

FRANK Of?

JANEEN The soul.

PINTO What kind of film do you use for that?

JANEEN The soul as it's seen on the faces of people, in the way they dress, the way they walk, how they eat. We think the soul is either a concept or some vapour-like substance. Oh no, it's real and as concrete as this desk. If the eyes are the mirror of the soul, then the eyes must be able to see it. The eyes. That's what I try to be. You're an artist. I know that.

PINTO Me?

JANEEN I saw one of your shows a few months ago.

FRANK Shows?

JANEEN Stand-up comedy's an art form.

FRANK Him? You? Pinto?

MAURICE You're a stand-up comic?

PINTO Sometimes.

FRANK I never knew that. You never said anything. You do think you're funny. Why were you keeping that from me? You're the one who leads a double life.

MAURICE You have to come to our show too. *(to FRANK)* You'll probably see my uncle at the opening. He says he knows you. Carlton Wilson.

FRANK I thought I saw some resemblance. We went to high school together. The next time you speak to him, say hello for me. And, oh yeah, say "Tweety Bird is missing a feather," he'll understand.

PINTO Hey that's the special code the Israeli Secret Service uses.

MAURICE Thanks very much for your time.

FRANK I'll let you know my decision very soon. But I'm telling you now, don't count on me being there so you should consider getting someone else.

MAURICE Isn't supporting Black aspirations part of your—?

JANEEN We understand. Thanks for your time.

FRANK Break a leg.

PINTO That's what you say to actors, not artists.

FRANK What do you say to them then?

PINTO I don't know. Break a lens?

JANEEN Thanks, and goodbye.

FRANK Goodbye.

MAURICE See you both at the show.

MAURICE and JANEEN exit.

FRANK They're so full of—

PINTO —enthusiasm.

FRANK What else are you keeping from me?

PINTO Nothing, really. I think you should speak at their opening.

FRANK What do you know?

PINTO Enough to see that it's a good idea.

FRANK I'm not interested in dealing with artists. They have their world, I have mine, and it's best that way. Those people.

PINTO Do you wanna know what I think?

FRANK No.

PINTO What I think is that you think those artists are silly posers who are wasting their time and should be doing something more real with themselves. You don't want to support them, okay, but don't look down on them. And I think you should consider going to the opening of the exhibition because it's a chance to meet people you might not otherwise, and a great opportunity to promote the Black Community Forum. You make lots of speeches and presentations, this is just one more. I thought you liked doing that kind of thing. There's bound to be some media people there as well. You should think about it. That's what I think.

FRANK You sure you don't want some of this sandwich?

Lights down on PINTO, up on JOHANNE.

JOHANNE Yes, yes, I agree, innocence is often the reason for misunderstanding.

FRANK Well, so that there is no further misunderstanding, it's very simple what I want you—

JOHANNE Very little in this world is simple, Monsieur Simmons. So when someone tells me that, it's usually because they don't really understand all—

FRANK Oh I understand per—

JOHANNE	The Conseil supports the arts and especially artists in this city in helping them to achieve their goals as much as possible. We don't allow or prevent them, we support them. We are not censors. In fact one of the show's artists is being considered for a *subvention* for a New York studio.
FRANK	I don't care about that – about one person. I care about the responsibility you have to our whole community. I don't want to hear about anything else.
JOHANNE	That depends on how you define that responsibility.
FRANK	Very simply. To make sure that the art you support does nothing to damage the Black community.
JOHANNE	I did not see anything in the Reflets Noirs exhibition that would damage your community.
FRANK	No, I suppose you wouldn't.
JOHANNE	What do you mean?
FRANK	You wouldn't feel the same way, you wouldn't be as insensitive if it were French Canadians portrayed in a negative light.
JOHANNE	What? What are you…?
FRANK	What if it were an exhibition showing Québécois eating Mae Wests* while playing the spoons? Maybe encouraging this kind of ridiculous exhibition, Black Reflections, serves your purpose.
JOHANNE	*Un'instant.* Purpose. *Ça, ça c'est trop.* I don't like what you're suggesting. *Non, pas du tout.* And now I am going to end this very unpleasant conversation.
FRANK	Go ahead, but I hope that you don't think this is the end of it.
JOHANNE	What I think is none of your business.
FRANK	We'll see about that.
JOHANNE	Goodbye, Monsieur Simmons. *(pronounces it Simons)*

---

* Mae West – a large chocolate cookie filled with cream.

FRANK It's Simmons.

JOHANNE Do you speak French?

FRANK Yes. *Bonjour.*

He hangs up. Lights out. Lights up on Comedy Club.

PINTO For the longest time Blacks and Jews have had a close but strange relationship. A book that came out a while back comes close to explaining that connection. This book strongly suggests that it was Nubians, Black Egyptian soldiers, who protected Jerusalem from being destroyed by invaders. If they hadn't, today there would be no Jerusalem, no Jews, no chopped liver, no Einstein, no polio vaccine, but also no Howard Stern. Oh well, small price to pay. And how did the Jews thank us, show their gratitude? They've been writing songs for us ever since. *Porgy and Bess*; early R & B; songs for the Drifters, Aretha Franklin, Billie Holiday, and on and on. A lot of the music that's defined and expressed the Black experience was written by Jews. Go know. You think those Nubians just marched away after saving the Jews? No sir. They stayed around to get a little freaky-freaky. Jews are part Nubian. Knowatimsayin'?

4th FRAME — THE ART OF BASKETBALL

Late Saturday morning. Small park with a basketball court. SHERMAN is standing directly beneath the basketball net. PINTO arrives. Throughout the scene they keep the basketball in near-constant motion, shooting at the hoop or each other, either to make a point or to emphasize their one-upmanship over the other.

PINTO Hey, white boy.

SHERMAN I keep tellin' you, I'm half-white.

PINTO Okay. Hey, confused boy.

SHERMAN You know what today is, don't you?

PINTO Get out from under there. And you're eating too! That's the Holy Hoop you're standin' under. Is nothing sacred to you?

SHERMAN Want some?

PINTO How cheap. You think talkin' 'bout food's gonna throw me off my game?

SHERMAN So?

PINTO I know what today is. Why do you think I'm here?

SHERMAN I wanna hear you say it.

PINTO And I want you to get out from under there.

SHERMAN Go 'head, say it. Say that this is Destiny Day.

PINTO The Galactic One-On-One Hoop Finals are mine.

SHERMAN Yup. Destiny Day. That's when the past and the present meet to change the future.

PINTO The only destiny goin' down here today is you meeting up with your inevitable loserhood.

SHERMAN Lose? Lose? No, no that can't be, that won't be. You see, when I win you win too. Yes you do, 'cause my winning means that you're gonna hafta do something you said you'd never do. That's the deal. It won't be easy, but it's part of learning to become a man. That lesson begins here today. You will thank me.

PINTO I'll thank you to up the fuck shut and get ready to play. Between your Oprahfying and Frank's ranting, my head feels like this basketball.

SHERMAN If Oprah married Deepak Chopra she'd be—

PINTO —unbearable.

SHERMAN Frank-enstein still giving you a hard time?

PINTO If I let him. Some of the work at the Association is boring so I treat him as a distraction, otherwise he'd be a real pain.

SHERMAN Good thing it's only for a little longer.

PINTO Everything's an argument with that man. I don't know if he realizes he pushes people away.

SHERMAN I know someone like that. Have you tried telling him?

PINTO I don't care enough.

SHERMAN You could be doing him a favour.

PINTO He's not the type, trust me. Too excitable or something. I don't know what it is, but—perfect example, the other day he went to a Black art show, really didn't like what he saw, lost control of his sphincter and let everybody have it.

SHERMAN Were you there?

PINTO No, I heard about it. I feel kinda responsible. I sort of persuaded him to go to the show.

SHERMAN You see, you can have an effect on him.

PINTO Anyway, I went yesterday to see what the noise was all about and I don't really know why he lost it. I mean yeah, you could say that some of the stuff in the show could be seen as glorifying pimps and thugs, or even be a politically incorrect way of looking at Black women, but—

SHERMAN —he could be right.

PINTO What?

SHERMAN Ya gotta be careful sometimes with images. Powerful stuff, man. The wrong images in the right eyes and who knows where that could lead.

PINTO Look at you. Porn-boy talkin' 'bout censorship.

SHERMAN I didn't say anything 'bout censorship. Why are you always putting words in my mouth?

PINTO So I can hear you say something intelligent.

SHERMAN I'm just saying you've got to be careful, 'specially when it comes to images of Black people.

PINTO We don't need to be protected, thank you very much, even by the likes of that half-Jewish, half-Irish Darwinian experiment called Sherman O'Donnell.

SHERMAN Bite of my potato bagel?

PINTO If we keep being afraid of how we're perceived, then we'll never get out from under, and nothin' will change. Thick skin beats small mind any day.

SHERMAN Maybe, but it doesn't stop bullets. Everybody's got their own soft spot, thick skin or not.

PINTO You know maybe Frank was so upset 'cause it was an art exhibition, you know, and that puts a different slide on things. Art's such a slippery thing.

SHERMAN Except when it comes to films. Now that's an art form. Did you ever see the original version of the film "Breathless" with Jean Paul Belmondo? "À Bout de souffle." Not that garbage version with Richard Gere. Belmondo. Now there was a guy who knew how to do things his way. He was in complete control. Man, was that guy cool. And the way he smoked cigarettes. The chicks didn't stand a chance.

PINTO That what you want?

SHERMAN I wanna be able to take a woman's breath away.

PINTO Don't shower for a week. That'll even cause her heart to skip a beat or two.

You think too much about "how to be" with women. Just "be." They're not looking for someone to take their breath away. They want someone who's going to give them reason to breathe deeply. You were talking before about the power of images, yeah maybe you're half right, but sometimes they only have as much power as you give them. What I'm sayin' is that it doesn't matter that you're weird and ugly, Sherman. That stuff doesn't bother women. As long as you're a good man, that's what counts for them. And I will say this about you, you are a mensch. So just be yourself, and everything'll be fine.

SHERMAN The day that I listen to anything you have to say about women is the day I turn my balls in 'cause I obviously don't need them anymore. What in anything I said to you sounded like I asked for your advice?

PINTO Not what you said, but how you said it. Think about it. And think about this: I don't know about movies as an art form, but I do know that Black people have given two art forms to the world: jazz and basketball. The world would be a sadder, lesser place without them, that's for sure. I don't even want to think about it.

SHERMAN Basketball was invented by a white man. A Canadian, in fact.

PINTO I ain't talkin' about the invention of it, I'm talkin' 'bout the playin' of it. A white guy may have invented it, but Black guys gave it its style. Without us the game would still be like curling. And to demonstrate to you what I mean, I want you to behold my artistry as I bring it down on your art-film-Belmondo-smokin'-white-Canadian-invented ass.

SHERMAN Half-white-Canadian-invented ass.

PINTO You're scared. No, no don't say anything. But I can always tell by the way you talk. I know you, Sherman O'Donnell. I know how you think. I know your strengths and your weaknesses. I know you. Look in my eyes. Look. What do you see? Yes, that's right, you see you. I got you right in here. Now stand back 'cause you smell of fear, and it's making it hard for me to breathe. I'm almost *à bout de soufflé*. So while I still can, let the Galactic One-On-One Hoop Finals begin.

SHERMAN Now I'm really gonna hafta beat you.

PINTO You can't. This is the Black man's game.

PINTO begins singing the chorus from R. Kelly's "I Believe I Can Fly." But just before he can demonstrate his artistry, SHERMAN stops him and whips off his outer layer of clothing to reveal an outfit that is hideously beautiful: Very long, baggy shorts in several different, clashing colours, one leg longer than the other, held up by rope that almost hangs down to the ground; a basketball T-shirt that has only one shoulder strap. On the front of it is a picture of SHERMAN and on the back the number 666. His outfit is a work of art. PINTO is frozen mid-shot, unable to move despite SHERMAN's beckoning him on. Lights down, up on Comedy Club.

Some of you must be confused what with all the name changes over the years. You're not sure what to call us or what you can call us. I think, why not something like Melanin-Enhanced or People of the Pigment. But no, it's African-American. This surprises me because most Blacks outside of Africa don't want anything to do with Africa. That's where the monkeys are. When a Black person wants to insult another Black person they'll say "You look like an African." Africa is far, far away and long, long ago, so to refer to oneself as an African-American must be for some reason other than proud identification. I figure it's to make white people think that we're ready to go back. Sorry, we're here to stay. That's unless they relocate the Los Angeles Lakers to Lagos. Can you imagine what it would do to the North American economy if we left? Thousands of people would lose their jobs; social unrest leading to wide-scale riots. Roving gangs of white looters break into swimwear stores, golf and bowling suppliers. And we'd be in Ghana, Kenya, Senegal, watching it on CNN—Crucial Nigger Network—shaking our heads saying "What's wrong with those people?"

Found art: the idea that art is everywhere if you care to look close enough. It's supposedly in the everyday things that we take for granted. I throw it away, it's junk: you find it, it's art. I was walking home the other day and I came across a rusted muffler tailpipe, so I picked it up and took it home. Cleaned it up a bit, painted it a luminous aquamarine, made a few holes in it and stuck some flowers in the holes. Then I strategically placed it in the northeast corner of my apartment opposite the door. Yin Yang with a little Feng Shui shit thrown in. The whole experience made me think what other lost things are out there waiting to be found, I mean besides love, the truth, and Cuba Gooding Jr.

Lights down.

5th FRAME — NIGGERIZING THE EYE

Sunday evening. MBA office. FRANK is working. There's a knock on the door.

FRANK Come in.

MAURICE enters.

What the hell are you doing here?

MAURICE I just wanted to clarify what it—

FRANK Don't want to hear anything you have to say. What a waste of talent.

MAURICE You misunderstood what we—

FRANK I misunderstood nothing. I know what I saw, and there's no mistaking that it's garbage.

MAURICE That's a little harsh, don't you think?

FRANK Not as harsh as some of those ugly images you're passing off as art. I'll say this for you and that other one, you sucked me in. "Your organization's and our exhibition's intentions are the same." The same? The same?

MAURICE They are. Look it's right up there on the wall, your—

FRANK Get away from there. You don't know what you're talking about. They couldn't be further apart. Worlds apart and now they've collided.

MAURICE Maybe if you came back and had a second look, then you might see what—

FRANK If you think I'm going to expose myself again to that—that—shit, then—

MAURICE Why are you so angry?

FRANK Because you've insulted me and Black people everywhere and you won't admit it. That's why.

MAURICE But to go to the Conseil and—

FRANK She went squealing to you, I see. I told you I was serious. I want that insult you call an art exhibition closed.

MAURICE I'm sorry you were insulted. That was not our intention. We simply thought that your presence at the opening would have been a good thing. A nice convergence. Too bad you feel otherwise, but the show will not be closed. You even admitted that you know nothing about art.

FRANK I do now. Thanks to you and your photographer girlfriend, it's all become quite clear to me.

MAURICE Then you should be able to see the irony.

FRANK The irony?

MAURICE Black Reflections/Reflets Noirs is an attempt to bring stereotypical images and notions of Black people out from behind the discursive background noise of hypocrisy and into the foreground of meaningful discourse.

FRANK What noise did you just make with your mouth? I don't speak art-ese.

MAURICE It's about niggerizing the eye.

FRANK What?

MAURICE Niggerizing the eye. The eye. The same way that we've taken over the word "nigger" and taken the wounding sting out of it, is the same way that you can change the way that we're seen. By taking control of the stereotyped images and using them in a certain way, little by little they lose their ugly power. Dignity through reappropriation.

FRANK Oh come on. You're talking to me, Frank Simmons, not some naïve, fawning interviewer. I live in the real world, not the let's-pretend art world. You don't make ugly beautiful by glorifying it.

MAURICE My work is not about glorifying anything. If that's what you saw then you missed the point.

FRANK That's right, I'm not hip enough to get it. Let me tell you what the point is, the point you missed. You take the sting out of nigger by not being a nigger. The moment Black people stop perpetuating the stereotyped images is the moment we regain our humanity. That's when Black becomes beautiful. Eliminating the stereotypes, not celebrating them. It's that simple. Here take this. Take it. It's a copy of the letter we've sent to the Black community inviting them to a public forum to discuss just such things. My invitation to you to enter the real world. Consider it your passport.

MAURICE I don't want to be a part of anything you're involved with.

Wait a minute. This isn't about art, and it's not even about stereotypes. This is about you. This is about you trying to make your mark. I just wish you hadn't chosen our tree to piss up against. Are you up for re-election?

FRANK Shut up. You're the one exploiting things for his own interests. Close down the exhibition.

MAURICE People have to see what we've done. It would be like me asking you to cover up that picture there of your family.

FRANK Don't you talk about that picture. You have no right. Don't even look at it. I said don't look at it.

MAURICE Easy, easy. It's just a picture.

FRANK Don't tell me what it is or isn't.

MAURICE Oh I see, but it's perfectly okay for you to tell people what's what.

FRANK I want you out of my office right now, Maurice Wilson. Door. Now.

MAURICE exits. Lights down. Lights up on the Funny Bones Comedy Club.

PINTO I've been thinking. You know we Black people have had to struggle with white people for so long. It's they who have supposedly made our lives so miserable. Now I say "supposedly," because I've been thinking, and what has become obvious to me is that our biggest problem is not white people. Our biggest problem is—our hair. That's right. Our hair. We don't know what the hell to do with it. Over the years we've straightened it, burnt it, fried it and even tried poisoning it. Anything to trick it into thinking that it was something other than what it really is. Then when none of that seemed to do the trick, we would shave it all off. That didn't solve the problem either. So when we got tired of fighting our own hair we decided to let it go native: the Afro. The big, fucked up Angela Davis 'fro. And for one brief shining moment, Black was beautiful. Then it got ugly again and the fight with our hair started all over. This time around we've added weaves, extensions, to the weapons. Then there are the dreadlocks. Maybe they're the solution. Who knows. As I said, our problem is not white people. Our problem is not having "white" hair. We come to terms with that, and we may well be on our way to some inner peace; better able to deal with white people. So I say to you, "Don't worry, be nappy."

6th FRAME — ON THE ROAD TO DAMASCUS

Wednesday evening. A cable TV studio. The hostess Joyce is unseen and unheard but is "present" between JANEEN and FRANK.

JANEEN Thank you very much, it's my first time and it's good to be here on "B is for Black." Yes I hope it won't be the last either.

FRANK That's right Joyce, many times and it's always a pleasure.

JANEEN Sure. My name is Janeen Danner and I'm a professional photographer. I trained here in Montreal, Toronto, and Rochester, New York. I do a little teaching, but most of my time is spent doing what I love most: capturing and documenting the world through the camera. Pictures tell stories, but they can also be the story as with Black Reflections/Reflets Noirs.

FRANK Frank Simmons, Executive Director of the Montreal Black Association. Three years now, but as you know, Joyce, I've been involved with the Black community for many, many years in one capacity or another. I'm also an accountant by training.

JANEEN No, I don't mind starting with me.

Yes, you could say I was shocked at his reaction. It seemed so… misinformed.

FRANK I'm not misinformed, you're misguided.

JANEEN He seems to think we're out to destroy, when in fact my work is about creating something.

FRANK Oh yeah, the old irony thing.

JANEEN There's nothing ironic about my photography.

FRANK Empowerment then: a woman's right to wear as little clothing as she wants. How else do you explain pictures of Black women wearing next to nothing and intentionally exposing themselves as they dance lewdly?

JANEEN Dancehall queens are a social phenomenon that—

FRANK Misleading.

JANEEN Dancehall queens are a social phenomenon that is about the breaking down of boundaries.

FRANK Where are they getting this stuff from?

JANEEN Get away from me.

FRANK I just wanted to see if I could see into your soul. Have you seen the pictures? Okay what do you think? I know you're the host, but your opinion matters.

JANEEN Don't look for other people to back you up.

FRANK I don't need backing up, you and your stupid ideas do. Besides, everyone out there knows the truth.

JANEEN I'll continue when he sits down.

When these women go to the club on a Saturday night, and yes, they are scantily dressed and yes, they do dance suggestively, I believe it's to say that they are not the least bit concerned with identity categories whose boundaries trap women, Black women. That's what I feel I've captured in my photos. If you look closely you can see the dissolving of those categories and boundaries.

FRANK plays to Joyce and then the camera.

FRANK This is – this is pure—

JANEEN Would you please sit down.

FRANK Don't tell me what to do.

Ask her about the wigs. I know you're the one doing the interview, but ask her, go ahead, ask her.

JANEEN It's okay, Joyce, I'll answer. Yes, they wear all kinds of wigs that are straight-haired and come in the most vivid, shock treatment colours that—

FRANK —make them look like fake white alien hookers.

JANEEN Stop interrupting me.

The wigs are a way of taking themselves and the dancehall setting outside of itself, the same way that "playin' mas" does at Carnival. Once you're outside the boundaries, the existing order is turned upside down for a little while. They're mocking themselves and expectations and I say good for them.

FRANK What do you mean that makes sense? I thought you wanted to be left out of it. You're supposed to be impartial, remember, so what are you doing taking sides?

Yes you are. It's ridiculous, you know that. "Playin' mas" my ass. Come on. Get up and show us.

JANEEN Touch me again and I'll slap you so hard you'll think you're white.

FRANK I have a 16-year-old daughter and what I want most for her is to be able to determine for herself what she wants, to be her own person. If you're watching, sweetheart, I love you. But the last thing I want is for her to think that she has to be like those dancehall queens to be true to herself. I would not want her to see your pictures.

JANEEN How do you know she hasn't? How do you know what your daughter does? Do you really know who she is?

FRANK That's none of your business.

JANEEN Then stay out of mine. And just in case you hadn't noticed, I'm a Black woman too and I wouldn't do anything that I thought was racist or misogynistic. You don't know anything about me. So don't you come in here and lecture me about the portrayal of Black women. You don't have the right to speak for women.

FRANK Because I'm a man?

JANEEN No, because you're an idiot.

FRANK Well this idiot knows enough when someone is spouting garbage and expecting me to swallow it.

JANEEN What you swallow is between you and your mouth.

FRANK Look, you people out there watching this show, I challenge you to prove that we're capable of seeing and presenting ourselves differently. Show me images other than hers. This is a challenge to you to show her that it's not 'bout playin' mas or any other such nonsense. So go ahead, show me other images. If we can't come up with ones that are opposite to hers, well, then, what's the point? I'll even resign as Executive Director of the Montreal Black Association.

JANEEN Good. In the meantime I've got a challenge for you. Come up with your own.

FRANK Own what?

JANEEN Images. I want you to show me other images. I want to see what you're talking about. I wanna see what you see.

FRANK This is not about me.

JANEEN Does that mean you won't accept my challenge?

FRANK Doesn't mean that at all. Not at all. I like a good challenge, even though this won't be much of one.

How hard can it be? Get camera, point, press button. The hardest part will be getting a grant. Ha, ha, ha.

JANEEN A little advice for you. It's not the camera that takes the picture. You take the picture with your eyes. Your imagination creates the image and your mind frames it. The camera simply lets others see what you did inside your head. It's the means by which you share your vision. Let me tell you something: the large part of the art of photography is in capturing what's not there, the unseen. Anybody can take a picture of the obvious.

FRANK Stop. Stop. Say that again.

JANEEN Don't touch me. What did I tell you about that?

FRANK Sorry, but say that again, that part about what's not there.

JANEEN That's what I said. Capture the unseen: what's outside the usual frame of things. But to do that means drawing on an imagination that has broken that frame. The photographer Diane Arbus said that a photograph is a secret about a secret.

FRANK Frame. Outside.

JANEEN What?

FRANK Broken. Secret. Unseen.

JANEEN Are you okay?

FRANK Imagination. Re-frame. Yes. Re-frame. Obvious.

JANEEN Is he okay? Is he having a stroke?

FRANK, as though in a trance, wanders out of the studio. Lights down. Lights up on Comedy Club.

PINTO Growing up in a West Indian family is not easy. From early, even though I was too young to be able to put it into words, I knew something was missing. It was only as I got older was I able to say what it was: sympathy. West Indian parents don't give their kids any sympathy whatsoever. Something bad happens to you and you turn to them for a little solace, understanding, forget it, you'll come away empty-handed and empty-hearted. You know how kids can be really quirky like not wanting the different foods on their plate to touch. "Don't let the peas touch the potatoes. Aghh, they touched" and the kid runs horrified from the table. White parent runs after them, "There, there, it's okay. That'll never happen again. Do you want some ice cream"? West Indian house: "Oh no, the peas touched the potatoes." Parent: *(in West Indian accent)* "Oh yeah, there's a problem? Let me fix it for you." Smash, smash, smash. "There. One love, one flavour. Now eat it." And don't even think about not eating it. No sympathy. No sensitivity. So frustrating, and it bugged me for the longest time. Then it struck me a little while ago that West Indian parents treat their kids like that as a way of preparing them for an insensitive world where as a Black person you can't expect to get a lot of sympathy. I can now appreciate what my parents were doing, 'cause otherwise I would be a very bitter person today. Once you've had your peas and potatoes smushed together right before your innocent child's eyes, well then, anything after that is a piece of cake.

Lights out.

7th FRAME — BREAKING THE FRAME

Slightly later same evening. Lights up on MBA office. FRANK enters and stops in front of the family picture on his desk. He stares at it for a while.

FRANK What a mess I've made.

Picks up the picture.

I thought you were stronger than that, I thought you could take it. I thought you were like me. I know I pushed and pushed, but it was only to make you better, to make you more than you were willing to settle for. And what happened? I pushed you right into the thing I was most afraid of and it sickened me. Right in here. It still hurts. I don't know how to get you back in the picture,

Germaine, but I'm going to try. Things are going to be different now.

He smashes the picture against the edge of the desk.

Break the frame in order to re-frame. Things have to be different.

Lights out.

Intermission.

ACT II

Lights up on Comedy Club.

PINTO Had a hard time getting here tonight. Kept getting stopped by the cops. Three times, and you know what that means. The last time a female cop pulls me over and says I made a lane change without using my flasher. Flasher? I said this is Quebec, you only use your flasher after you hit somebody to indicate which direction the body was thrown in, and the hazards if the body is still sprawled over the windshield and you can't see where you're going. Flashers? Please.

Most orgasms last for seven seconds. Seven seconds. Yeah they do. I've timed them. All that huffin' and puffin'—not to mention the planning and scheming—for seven seconds of screeching and whimpering. Oh well. But it's probably a good thing that it doesn't last much longer 'cause you've lost seven seconds of dignity, and higher brain functions. Seven seconds of that is enough.
I recently heard that pigs have orgasms that last for thirty minutes. Thirty minutes. The pigs. No wonder bacon tastes so good. If I had orgasms that lasted 30 minutes, I'd wanna eat me too.

He takes a piece of paper from his pocket.

The Tele-personal ads. Let me read you one:

Single professional Black male in his mid-thirties. Enjoys good conversation, and the finer things in life, such as moonlight walks, candlelight dining by the fireplace, bowling. I don't think so. A brother did not write that. That's a white guy trying to pass himself off as Black. Moonlight walks. Bowling. That's definitely a white guy. How can I be so certain? Well, that's because most people secretly want to be one of three things they're not: Italian, Black or a woman. A brother bowling? The whole bowling motion is at odds with the way Black people carry themselves. You've seen the way we walk. All of that runs counter to the bowling motion. It's just not in our musculature. White people don't walk like we do. At least they're not supposed to, and when they do it catches your attention, doesn't it? The only way Black people would go bowling is if they could look and act like John Turturro in "The Big Lebowski." And besides, whenever a Black person has tried to bowl they've ended up with a strange desire afterwards to listen to Abba or watch Walton re-runs. I'm issuing a warning right now to Black people: repeated attempts to bowl can result in severe muscular discomfort and a bad record collection. You've been warned.

Lights down.

8th FRAME — THE CAUCASIAN CONSULTANT

Late Tuesday morning. JANEEN and MAURICE at the exhibition.

JANEEN I'm hungry. What do you want to have for lunch?

MAURICE You're hungry and you ask me what I want to eat. That must be female-speak for: go get me some food.

JANEEN Very good. You're learning. Next week we'll cover double negatives in the future tense.

MAURICE As long as it doesn't mean no sex for weeks to come.

JANEEN To be honest, Frank Simmons has done us a bit of a favour.

MAURICE Just how?

JANEEN Look around.

MAURICE I don't care if he's brought more attention to the show. It's for the wrong reasons.

JANEEN What we wanted was for people to see our work. Look, they're seeing.

MAURICE But because of that ignorant man, just what are they seeing?

JANEEN We've done our job. The rest is up to the people who come to see. Look at that woman in the green dress looking at your installation, the way she steps away from it then gets closer, then steps away again. Who knows what she makes of it, but her body language says that it means something to her – she's been affected. Maurice, you've done your job. Who cares why all these people are here. They're here and they probably wouldn't have come otherwise. Forget about Frank Simmons. I have. Don't worry, he's not going to affect your chance for the studio.

MAURICE It's not about that.

JANEEN Yes it is. Be honest with yourself.

MAURICE It's not about the studio. It's about artistic freedom. It's about Black people holding Black people back. And it's about letting people who don't have a clue know you're on to them.

JANEEN So what do you want to do?

MAURICE I don't know. I'll think of something. Don't you worry.

JANEEN He probably just needs a good enema.

SHERMAN enters.

SHERMAN Hi. You two are the artists, right?

They both nod.

Amazing stuff.

JANEEN Thank you. How did you hear about the show?

SHERMAN Through a friend. But once the controversy started I knew I had to come.

JANEEN I told you.

SHERMAN To see for myself. To see if the show was safe.

MAURICE Safe?

SHERMAN Safe for Black people.

JANEEN Safe for Black people?

SHERMAN I had to see if what you've done here was going to make life easier or harder for Black people in the long run.

MAURICE Why should that matter to you?

SHERMAN It should matter to everyone.

MAURICE Yeah, in the ideal world that we don't live in.

SHERMAN I don't know why, it just matters to me.

JANEEN Your conclusion?

SHERMAN It's going to make it harder for white people. It's going to make it harder for them to decide what's real, the person or the image. More confusion and ambiguity, you know. But I think that's ultimately a good thing because it'll force them to question some things. It's made me examine some of my assumptions.

JANEEN But I have this feeling you're not like most people.

SHERMAN So I've heard.

I can see why some people would have a problem with the show, but I'm glad it wasn't shut down. It woulda been a major drag if I didn't get to see it.

MAURICE And it isn't gonna be closed down either.

SHERMAN Well if there's a threat I know how you can deal with it.

Your silence encourages me so I'm going to tell you. Turn the tables. Protest the protester. Criticize the critic. It's the perfect artist's revenge.

SHERMAN acts out the following as he speaks:

I remember when I was in high school a bunch of us demonstrated in front of a company that made pesticides. We walked up and down with signs held high, chanting: "We'll pester you until there's no more pesticides," and "Pests inside, pests outside, down with pesticides." I think we sang "We Shall Overcome" and "Kumbaya." My joy was short-lived because my dad worked for the company and when he saw me he came out and punched me, knocked me to the ground and went back inside. At dinner that evening he asked me how my day was. What my dad didn't know was that it was my mom who organized the demonstration. That evening at dinner she got up from her seat, went over to where my dad was sitting and punched him. Knocked him to the floor and then asked him if he wanted seconds. Anyways, it's just a suggestion.

JANEEN Thanks.

SHERMAN You're welcome. I've gotta run. You guys have really done something here. It's mango. Ripe mango. See ya.

He exits. MAURICE and JANEEN are left standing looking at each other in bewilderment. Lights down.

9th FRAME — BLACKOUT

Saturday morning. Black Community Forum. FRANK is up on the podium.

FRANK Thank you very much, Florence. Thank you for those kind words about me and thank you for that enlightening opening address. As Chairperson of the Board of the Montreal Black Association your observations about the current state of affairs are both critical and timely. And most of all, thanks to all of you for being here. I look out and I see many familiar and unfamiliar faces. I see you, Carlin and Gwen and Thomas, people who have done so much for our community. Of course I see my lovely wife Dorothy. But most importantly I see the faces of our youth who are both the hope for the future and our hope that the past won't be forgotten. To all of you, welcome to the very first Black Community Forum. I almost said "The First Annual Black Community Forum," but that suggests that we are doomed to useless, eternal attempts to change our present circumstances.

If I thought that that was the slightest possibility, so much time and effort organizing would not have been spent. Things can change. Every item on the agenda for this weekend is important. However, I have recently become aware of something that I cannot keep to myself. I believe that it will shed an illuminating light on everything that will be said over the next two days.

The indignities, the difficulties, the abuses our community and Black people everywhere have suffered have many causes and roots, but I'm afraid that one of the main reasons behind our situation has to do with how we identify ourselves and are identified by others. You've all seen the cowboy movies where the good guy wears the white hat and the bad guy the black hat. Or in the cartoons there's Snow White, the perfect symbol of purity and goodness, done in by the black-hearted Queen. Black humour. Blackmail. Black Monday. Blacklist. Black mark. Black death.

And there are lots more. Black is, and has for a long time been, associated with all that is bad, dirty and evil. It is the underside of things, that which has to be avoided or despised. Black is bad and therefore if you're Black you're bad, and if you're bad then it becomes easier to do bad things and easier for others to do bad things to you. The Gospel according to St. John says: "And in the beginning was the Word." True. Equally true is that in the end there is the image. What the word "black" stands for is bad and is not the image we can afford to carry around anymore. Its continued existence as an identifier will only allow for us to be mistreated both from inside and outside our community.

He moves away from the lectern.

Oprah Winfrey. Very successful woman. Very rich woman.The highest female income earner in entertainment in the United States. Know why? Because she's managed to sell herself as a woman, not a Black woman, just a woman. When you see her you don't think Black, you think person. They're even calling Chicago "Oprahville" now.

He moves into the audience.

I see many of you frowning and shifting uncomfortably in your seats. I understand, but I have a little bit more to say and it comes in the form of a request. First, do not dismiss what I've said, please give it some consideration just in case I'm right and if I am, then do this for me, no, not for me, for yourself, for all of us: stop using the word "Black" to identify yourself. It does not describe me, or you, or you. So, instead of Black, may I humbly offer as a replacement, God's Colour. That's right. God's Colour. Because that's who we truly and rightfully are. Go ahead, laugh and hoot if you want. God's Colour Community Forum. I think it has a nice ring to it. Anyway that's all I have to say, so thank you for listening.

Lights out. Lights up on the Comedy Club.

PINTO If you've been wondering about God's gender, I've figured it out. The vagina is proof that God is a woman. The penis is proof that she has a sense of humour. *(mouths:)* Think about it.

10th FRAME — QUESTIONABLE CIRCUMSTANCES

Early Saturday afternoon. Same basketball court from earlier scene. PINTO and SHERMAN are playing.

PINTO Okay, just one more game. The dad-man and I are going to my uncle's place to help him fix his garage door or something.

SHERMAN Alright, I'll make this mercifully quick.

He begins dribbling the ball and is about to shoot but is interrupted by PINTO.

PINTO The bet's off.

SHERMAN What?

PINTO The bet's off. I can't go through with it. I've been thinking and I can't do it.

SHERMAN That's the problem right there. You've been thinking. The bet's not off. There was a deal and I expect you to stick to it.

PINTO I know there was a deal and you know me to be a man of my word, but I'm going to have to break this one.

SHERMAN What do you think this is, the NBA? There's no breaking of deals. A bet's a bet. If it were reversed you wouldn't let me out of it, and I wouldn't expect you to. The loser of the Galactic One-On–One Hoop Finals was going to have to do something he said he'd never do. You knew the conditions.

PINTO I know but—

SHERMAN I know you know, and that's where it ends. The outcome has already been settled and I'm holding you to it. Just be glad you don't have to do the food thing.

PINTO I know but—

SHERMAN We shook.

PINTO Okay, okay. But I don't see why you gotta be so anal.

SHERMAN 'Cause you're being a rectum.

FRANK enters.

FRANK Pinto.

PINTO Frank? What – how come you're here? What a coincidence.

FRANK No coincidence. I came to talk to you.

PINTO Me? How'd you know I'd be here?

FRANK Hello, my name's Frank Simmons.

PINTO Oh sorry. Frank this is Sherman.

SHERMAN Pleased to meet you. Pinto's talked a lot about you.

PINTO Well, not that much, just a little.

SHERMAN No, more than that. Is that what I think it is?

FRANK I don't know what you're thinking, but it's a camera, a Po—

SHERMAN —laroid. Oh baby. I saw one of those at my grandad's house once. What a Smithsonian. Can I see it?

PINTO You're taking pictures?

FRANK I'm trying. Not being entirely successful, but I'm trying. I'm sorry to interrupt your game, but there's something I wanted to ask you.

PINTO Does it have to do with yesterday, because I can tell you right now that your speech grabbed everyone by the short and curlies, and there were lots of short and curlies in that room.

SHERMAN I heard about what you said. Wish I'd been there.

FRANK What I have to ask you is related to yesterday. Your answer is important to me.

PINTO Okay.

FRANK What would you look like if you weren't Black?

PINTO Ha, ha, ha. That's very funny. I'm gonna have to work that into one of my routines. Very funny.

FRANK I'm serious.

SHERMAN I like the question.

PINTO That's because it doesn't make any sense.

FRANK Think about it.

PINTO Think about what? There's nothing to think about. I can't even imagine.

SHERMAN It's like asking someone: What's the sound of one lip talking?

PINTO What in the name of Lebron James are you on about? Look, I am Black, my father is Black, my mother is Black, my sister is Black, even our dog is black. I can't imagine being or wanting to be anything else. I like being Black. And don't expect me to refer to myself as God's Colour either. What if someone doesn't believe in God?

FRANK Then they've got more to worry about than the colour of things.

PINTO With all due respect, I have to tell you I think it's naïve. Sometimes attitudes are so deep that language can't even get there with a shovel.

FRANK I am not a naïve man. It's just a good place to start to change those attitudes.

PINTO Some things have got to change, but that's not how you go about it. After all the work you put into the Forum I don't understand how you could have said what you did and just left. I thought the Forum was going to be your legacy?

FRANK I feel that what I said yesterday is my legacy. I have nothing more to add.

PINTO I really don't know why you're doing this, and is that what you really came here to ask me?

FRANK Yes, why else?

PINTO I don't know. It's just that you track me down to ask me that strange question and—

FRANK It's a very important question that may not have an answer but I believe it has to be asked, and I wanted to try it out on you before I ask other people.

PINTO Other people?

FRANK Yes. I'm going to ask a whole bunch of people: If you weren't Black, what would you be doing that you aren't now?

SHERMAN Wow. That's a good one.

FRANK And I'm going to take pictures of their answers.

PINTO Questions. Pictures. What's happened to you? You're setting yourself up for a lot of ridicule. You should have heard the things people were saying after you left.

FRANK I can imagine.

PINTO Some people even think you should resign.

FRANK I don't care. What I'm really asking people to question is if being Black is limiting the way they lead their lives.

Anything to get them to see if they've squeezed that life into a frame that then traps them.

PINTO I don't know. This is all a bit much. I have to tell you, what you're doing, saying – I think you mean well, but it's beyond naïve, it's a bit of a joke.

FRANK You think I'm a joke. Is that what you've thought about me all along? Is that what you've been telling your friend here?

PINTO That's not what I said. I didn't say you were a joke, I—

FRANK Don't split split hairs with me. Be a man and stand behind what you say or don't say it at all.

PINTO I know what I said. You, as usual, only hear yourself.

FRANK Am I a joke?

PINTO Things are not going to change for Black people—

FRANK Am I a joke? Answer me.

PINTO Right now, yes. So I think you should leave. We're trying to have some fun here.

FRANK You think that just because you're a comedian everything's a big—

PINTO What the fuck is your problem?

FRANK You.

PINTO Are you gone yet? Is he gone yet?

FRANK storms off, stops and he and PINTO stare at each other for a while until FRANK turns and leaves.

SHERMAN That was interesting.

PINTO Fuckin' asshole. See what I mean.

SHERMAN Hey, where you goin'? We got another game.

PINTO Play it yourself.

PINTO leaves, but before he's out of earshot:

SHERMAN You might have won. Finally.

Lights down. Lights slowly up to reveal FRANK wandering the streets looking for people to question and photograph.

11th FRAME — THE BIG PICTURE

Late Saturday afternoon. MBA office. PINTO bursts in and almost knocks FRANK over.

PINTO Oh shit. I didn't think you'd be here.

PINTO turns to leave.

FRANK Wait.

PINTO Gotta go.

FRANK I want to say—

PINTO I don't want to hear—

FRANK —hear me out. A moment please. Being told that I'm a joke is—

PINTO I didn't say you—

FRANK —it's painful for me. It cuts deeply. Used anywhere in my vicinity and I – I…. That's where you come in, sort of.

PINTO I told you—

FRANK I know what you said this afternoon. I heard you, but I also heard someone else.

Whenever we had an argument, and that was often, my son would tell me that I was a big joke. But he would say it in a way that would make me feel small. So I'd yell louder and he would just laugh. I felt stupid and lost in those moments.

PINTO I wasn't doing any of that.

FRANK I know. Sort of. Things got a little confused for me. I started to blur the line between you and him.

FRANK goes over to his desk.

You remember that picture of my family that I used to have over here?

PINTO Yes.

FRANK I broke it. Best thing I've done in a long time. I don't know if you ever looked closely at it, but if you did you might have noticed something a little peculiar. Dorothy is looking at something that isn't there. What she was looking at was our son Germaine. I had him digitally removed from the picture when he left home, turned his back on us and joined that goddamn gang. Dorothy doesn't know I took him out of the picture, but I had to. Two years ago he took himself out of our lives, so I took him out of the picture. Germaine, my 19-year-old son, gone.

PINTO Where is he now?

FRANK Out there somewhere, and I want him back. I want him home where he belongs. But you were right here and so I thought that if I could—

PINTO That's why you invited me for dinner.

FRANK I thought that if I could bring you home then maybe you could—

PINTO —fill in the picture.

FRANK Sort of.

PINTO I gotta go. I can pick up my things another time.

FRANK This may sound strange, what with all I said and everything, but the dinner invitation was for this evening. It's still open.

PINTO I know. I remember. But I can't.

FRANK I don't want you to be—

PINTO I wish I could but I just can't.

FRANK Dorothy will be disappointed. I'll be disappointed.

PINTO Tell her an emergency came up.

FRANK Tell me the truth. Be honest with me. I told you.

PINTO I – can't eat – with – I can't eat when there are other people around. I can't eat in front of other people. Going out to eat is out for me; restaurants and that kind of thing, I can't. I just can't do it.

FRANK You're kidding me, right? A joke.

PINTO No joke. I can only eat with my family or when I'm alone. Have you ever seen me eat anything here? No you haven't, because I haven't.

FRANK I don't understand.

PINTO It's—

FRANK How long? Since when?

PINTO A few years now.

FRANK That long.

PINTO I was eating my lunch in the cafeteria, a tuna fish sandwich, it just wouldn't go down. It felt like everyone was watching me chew and swallow and I became so self-conscious I couldn't swallow. I had to go to the bathroom to spit it out. Ever since then I can't eat if there's anyone around.

FRANK Except your family.

PINTO Yeah.

FRANK This is unbelievable. It must be – horrible – I mean, can't imagine what it must be like. You should have said something.

PINTO I don't talk about it. You don't talk about your son. I don't talk about it. It's an anxiety thing. I get anxious, you know, nervous.

FRANK Anxious about what?

PINTO Just anxious.

FRANK I'm really sorry to hear this. My God, you stand up on a stage in front of perfect strangers, tell jokes, try to make them laugh, put yourself on the line. Talk about being singled out, and yet you can't eat sitting down with four other people.

PINTO Not the same thing.

FRANK Oh, come on.

PINTO I'm telling you it's not. When I'm on stage it's not me the audience is looking at, it's the comedian Pinto. I can hide behind that. But when I'm not on stage, constantly being stared at as a visible minority member – well a whole lifetime of that was too much for me. I became too self-conscious.

FRANK That's no reason not to eat.

PINTO You know what I'm talking about. And being called God's Colour isn't going to change any of that. Every Black person has to deal with it in their own way. What's yours?

I'll pick my things up another time.

He exits. Lights down.

12th FRAME — TAKEN FOR GRANTED

Monday morning. JOHANNE Tétreault's office. There is a knock on her door.

JOHANNE *Entrez.*

FRANK enters.

Est-ce-que je peux vous aider?

FRANK I'm Frank Simmons.

JOHANNE So that's what you look like. What are you doing here?

FRANK I want you to—

JOHANNE *Un instant.* You want. You want. You come in here in my office with wants. No it doesn't work that way. In my office it's what I want, and I want you out of here.

FRANK Not before I say what I have to say.

JOHANNE There is absolutely nothing I want to hear from you. I've already heard enough.

FRANK No you haven't.

JOHANNE *Pardon?* I want you to come over to this window. Yes. You over here. Come here. *Venez ici, j'ai dit.* Now look out and tell me what you see.

FRANK What I see?

JOHANNE That's what I said. Look. There.

FRANK I don't know. People.

JOHANNE Good. And what are these people doing?

FRANK Just – sitting around.

JOHANNE That's right. Just sitting around and if you look closely—go ahead—you can see that the look on their faces says that they don't give a shit about you and your wants. And, Mr. Simmons, I don't either. So take them elsewhere.

FRANK I would like you to listen to what I have to say.

JOHANNE I don't listen to people who insult me and then hang up.

FRANK Oh you're upset about that. All right, I apologize.

JOHANNE Whether or not you mean it.

FRANK I have a request—

JOHANNE You have a lot of nerve.

FRANK Little happens otherwise.

Beat.

JOHANNE *Je vous écoute. Trente seconds.*

FRANK Since you won't close the Black Reflections show or distance yourself from it, I want—

JOHANNE What did I tell you about that?

FRANK Would you please consider supporting an alternate show that provides a different view of things.

JOHANNE Alternate show? Different view? What—

FRANK An exhibition of pictures that counters those unacceptable ones.

JOHANNE You should know we don't provide support just like that. It doesn't work that way. I hope you're finished speaking because your *trente seconds* are up and I've finished listening.

FRANK But you didn't hear me.

JOHANNE No, no, you did not hear me. We don't—

FRANK Look I do know how you operate. This is a special circumstance.

JOHANNE You think everything about you is special. I don't agree, and I am very busy, so if you don't mind—

FRANK I mind very much, that's why I took pictures of my people that offer another perspective. It's not that they're my pictures, it's that it's another perspective. They should be seen.

JOHANNE As you say. But as I said, that's not how we operate.

FRANK But you do operate in a responsible manner, and it's your responsibility to—

JOHANNE No it's not our responsibility at all. If you think your pictures should be seen then fine, go show them, but we don't have any responsibility to you. My responsibility is to this *organisme* and its integrity, and I don't like— I dislike very much—anyone playing with that. I dislike that almost as much as someone playing with my personal integrity. And you did that when we spoke on the telephone.

FRANK I did no such thing.

JOHANNE I heard your not-so-subtle accusation of racism. Let me—

FRANK You heard what?

JOHANNE I know what I heard. Let me tell you, you know nothing about me.

FRANK I didn't say I did.

JOHANNE Look at this picture. Go ahead look. What do you see?

FRANK It's you.

JOHANNE And?

FRANK And another woman.

JOHANNE And? And?

FRANK You're holding hands.

JOHANNE That's right. But you forgot something else.

FRANK She's… Bla… God's Colour.

JOHANNE *Pardon?*

FRANK Nothing.

JOHANNE What's wrong?

FRANK You're—

JOHANNE You're never at a loss for words. *Allez-y.* Say it.

FRANK Lesbian.

JOHANNE *Bon.* In future before you make accusations, think of this picture. About your pictures, take them to Reflets Noirs and see if they feel they have a responsibility to show them.

FRANK That's not helpful.

JOHANNE It's the best I can do for you. *En tout cas,* Monsieur Simmons, I really am very busy and I have a meeting.

FRANK You pronounced my name right.

JOHANNE No, I didn't pronounce it wrong. There is a difference.

Lights down. Lights up on the Funny Bones Comedy Club.

PINTO I get it now. Abstract expressionism, representational art, conceptual art, performance pieces, they're the art world's niggers. Outside, different, threatening, refusing to know their place, but at the same time necessary, no, essential to mainstream art. Slowly, quietly, mainstream art borrows from the outsiders and incorporates what it's comfortable with and then says: "Look at what I've done. Good, eh?" Mainstream art needs all that unacceptable, threatening shit, otherwise it would die. So all you niggers out there, the world needs us. As you leave here tonight keep repeating to yourself: I am a work of art, I am needed. Now some of you are works in progress but I can still see your beauty, so remember: I am a work of art.

13th FRAME — IMAGINE THAT

Thursday afternoon. FRANK enters the Black Reflections/Reflets Noirs exhibition.

MAURICE Well, well, look who's here.

FRANK puts a package on the table in front of MAURICE and JANEEN.

FRANK I would like you to look at these.

JANEEN What are you doing here?

FRANK Look at them.

MAURICE Door.

FRANK I want you to look at these pictures, that's what I'm doing here.

MAURICE Did you hear me?

JANEEN I think you should leave.

FRANK They're what you challenged me to. "Other images."

MAURICE I don't care what they are. Take them and leave. Now.

FRANK I really would like you to look at them. You'll be surprised.

MAURICE sweeps them onto the floor.

MAURICE I don't like surprises.

FRANK picks them up and places them back on the table.

Are you deaf along with being ignorant? I'm telling you—

FRANK Just look at them. What are you afraid of?

MAURICE What I'll do if you don't get your sorry ass out of here now.

FRANK I will. Just look at them.

JANEEN Then you leave.

MAURICE *(to JANEEN)* Don't touch them.

JANEEN Don't you tell me what to do.

FRANK I heard what you said about "capturing what's not there."

JANEEN And these pictures are—

FRANK —the result.

MAURICE What is this bullshit?

JANEEN Hang on.

MAURICE Don't you tell me what to do.

FRANK I'm going to tell you both what to do.

JANEEN & MAURICE *(simultaneously)* No you're not.

FRANK Add my pictures to your show. The contrast will create a real dialogue. People can decide for themselves. Alone, your pictures and video are missing a context. My pictures provide that context. Put mine alongside yours. One set of images speaking to or about the other. If you're honest with yourselves you'll admit that contrasting images play off each other so that each says something they couldn't say on their own. And if you're true artists you'll want to hear what it is they have to say. You call this Black Reflections, then let it be a real reflection.

MAURICE Finished? I said are you finished. Doesn't matter, I'm throwing you out right now.

JANEEN Maurice.

MAURICE Maurice nothing, I've had it with this—

FRANK Did you speak to Germaine?

MAURICE What?

FRANK Did you speak to him?

MAURICE Who?

FRANK Germaine Simmons. My son.

MAURICE What about him?

FRANK I wanna know if you spoke with him when you videotaped him. When you videotaped those gang members and wannabe thugs did you speak with him or did you simply take video pictures of him and not ask him any questions about himself. Whether he was happy or not, whether he missed his family, if he knows he's broken his mother's heart, and that his family should be the only gang he needs. Did you? Tell me, did you?

MAURICE I knew it. I knew it was something personal. All puffed up about insulting the Black community. Bullshit man. It was just about you all along. I told you, Janeen. I was right. How sad you let your personal life get in my—our—way, and it was just about you and your failure as a father.

MAURICE sweeps the pictures onto the floor again. FRANK picks them up once more and places them back onto the table.

You're no artist. You're just a sad excuse for a community leader and a man who can't even keep his family together, how the hell—

JANEEN Okay, Maurice, that's enough.

MAURICE Whose side are you on?

JANEEN You've made your point.

MAURICE Take your pictures and get the fuck out of here.

FRANK Please. Show them. They're important. Please.

This is not about me. This is about us. Forget how you feel about me and look at them with the eyes of the artist you call yourself. If you can't do that—

MAURICE is about to throw the pictures at FRANK, JANEEN stops him.

JANEEN I'll take them. *(to FRANK)* Leave.

MAURICE What—?

JANEEN Leave now.

FRANK exits. MAURICE grabs a garbage pail and holds it in front of JANEEN.

MAURICE If you look at those pictures, Mr. Surface and his work are outta here.

Lights down.

14th FRAME — THE RESPONSIVE STIMULUS

Two weeks later, Friday evening. Association office. PINTO and FRANK are working around the office.

PINTO I've cleaned up the files on the computer, here's the list of potential contributors, and if you could sign this, I need it for the university.

FRANK I really enjoyed my university days.

PINTO Thank you.

FRANK The Board will be sending you an official letter of appreciation. I wrote it.

PINTO I should have my organizational assessment finished by next week. I'll send it in as soon as it's done.

FRANK No hurry. The new Executive Director, whoever that is, is going to have a lot of dossiers and other things to deal with.

PINTO So what's next?

FRANK Focus on my accounting practice. I'll still come around here once in a while, kind of as a consultant. Whether they want it or not.

Hey, it's Friday evening. You must have plans.

PINTO Yeah. Going out.

FRANK Where?

PINTO Out. My buddy Sherman's coming by to pick me up.

FRANK Out.

PINTO Yeah. Out.

FRANK Where, out?

PINTO Nowhere special.

There's a knock on the door.

Come in.

SHERMAN enters.

SHERMAN Hi everybody.

FRANK Good to see you again.

SHERMAN Likewise. Ready?

PINTO Yeah, just let me put these things away.

SHERMAN I heard you're starting a new life.

FRANK On many levels.

SHERMAN Renewal is a good thing. I think it's important to re-invent yourself every now and then. Don't you agree?

PINTO I wouldn't know.

SHERMAN Oh, but you will.

FRANK What's in that—?

PINTO Okay, I'm ready. Let's go.

SHERMAN It's a—

PINTO C'mon, we're gonna be late.

SHERMAN We got time.

FRANK So, what's in that very round—?

PINTO It's not important. C'mon, let's—

FRANK Maybe not, but I'm just curious, unless he doesn't want to tell me.

SHERMAN A bowling ball.

FRANK A bowling ball?

SHERMAN Yup. Got my own.

FRANK And you're going bowling.

SHERMAN We are.

FRANK Pinto's going bowling? With you? On a Friday night? What is this? You bowling? What else are you keeping from me?

PINTO Nothing, really.

SHERMAN He's a natural. I can spot 'em.

PINTO Shut up.

FRANK No, no, speak.

SHERMAN Well, you see—

PINTO —we had this little bet and he—

SHERMAN —won. Yes I did. Beat him in the Galactic One-On-One Hoop Finals. The loser would have to do something he said he'd never do. And now your lovely assistant's going bowling.

FRANK You lost at basketball?

SHERMAN Badly.

PINTO Hey, it was close.

SHERMAN For a little while.

FRANK To him? I'm sorry, I didn't mean that the way it sounded.

SHERMAN That's okay. Looks can be deceiving.

FRANK When I asked you to imagine not being Black, I didn't mean for you to have to lose at basketball.

PINTO It was what he was wearing.

FRANK And what would you have to do if you lost?

SHERMAN Go on a date with someone from the "Tele-Personals."

PINTO Damn, I wish that had happened. Would've liked to have seen that.

SHERMAN You're not too late. I decided that you shouldn't be the only one having a "life-expanding experience." When I let myself think about what you said about "being myself" with women, I realized that I did need more spontaneity in that area of my life. I needed to trust that I was enough, so I thought a good test for that would be going on a date with someone from the "Tele-Personals." And that's what I'm gonna do next week. As I said, it's important to renew yourself every now and then.

PINTO Yeah, yeah, yeah, but who is she? What are you gonna do?

SHERMAN Going to the movies. "À Bout de souffle."

FRANK Is it supposed to be good?

PINTO Don't get him started.

SHERMAN Your questions got me thinking about if I was only doing things because of the way I defined myself, you know, this is Sherman O'Donnell, and the rest isn't.

PINTO You listened to my good advice because of his bizarre questions?

SHERMAN nods.

Pardon my Hebrew, but that's fucked up. You're weirder than I thought possible.

FRANK Can I see that?

SHERMAN Sure.

FRANK Nice colours. I thought they were supposed to be Black.

PINTO I've got a question for you.

FRANK Okay.

PINTO If Black people stop being Black, then who are white people going to imitate?

SHERMAN Why are you looking at me? I'm an original. I don't need to imitate nobody.

PINTO Then on the court stop trying to do my patented seahorse shot. Don't try it again 'cause you could hurt yourself and you look stupid doin' it too.

SHERMAN You wanna see imitation? The next time we play I will show you my imitation of a certain God's Colour guy who thinks he can play basketball.

PINTO I can't do this. I can't, no, I won't go bowling. It's not me, it's not for me. The whole thing was stupid to begin with. I'm not going. It's all wrong. I don't belong in a bowling alley. A bowling alley. Have you ever been inside one of those places? It's not me. It's so – I don't fit.

FRANK Are you sure?

PINTO Very.

FRANK I respect your feelings and of course it's your decision, but I think it would be good for you to go.

PINTO Let's get this over with.

SHERMAN Ah, man, you're gonna have the time of your life.

PINTO No, you're gonna have the time of your life seeing me embarrass myself.

SHERMAN Yeah that too.

PINTO C'mon. But those bowling shoes. Not on these feet.

FRANK I always knew you'd end up in the gutter. Ha, ha, ha.

PINTO Frank. You're not a joke but you're not funny.

SHERMAN I thought it was funny.

PINTO Are you coming or not?

PINTO and SHERMAN exit. FRANK mimics the motions of a bowler, then shrugs his shoulders and shakes his head as he doesn't get it. Lights down.

15th FRAME — INSIDE OUT

Saturday evening. Black Reflections/Reflets Noirs exhibition. JANEEN is standing by herself slightly away from the crowd. FRANK comes rushing over to her.

FRANK This is something. Really something. I don't know – I can't thank you enough. Oh sorry, I'm not supposed to touch you. I forgot.

JANEEN When you first came in here with your pictures you said that images should speak to each other. When you said it I knew it was right, you were right. And they do. Loudly, clearly and eloquently. It's beautiful. They think so too. The people. Look at them.

FRANK But it cost you.

JANEEN What doesn't?

FRANK No, no, really cost you.

JANEEN It was such a strange feeling being put into the kind of situation that you always played out in your mind, wondering what you would do if you had to make a difficult choice – a choice, between your head and your heart, your principles and your feelings. And there I was living it out for real. Did that ever happen to you?

FRANK Oh yes.

JANEEN And what did you do?

FRANK Not the right thing.

JANEEN I miss him. It hurts.

FRANK Yes.

They spend a few moments in silence.

You only gave me the first half of that quotation, not the second.

JANEEN Which quotation?

FRANK "A photograph is a secret"—

JANEEN —"about a secret."

FRANK "The more it tells you, the less you know." I don't know that I agree with that part. Look at these pictures, yours and mine. They say so much about the range of possibilities our people have open to them. That I know.

JANEEN If they want it.

JOHANNE enters.

JOHANNE *Félicitations.*

JANEEN Merci.

JOHANNE I like the new name. This is us/Ça c'est nous.

FRANK Her idea.

JANEEN It made more sense, that's all.

JOHANNE I'm sorry to hear about what happened with Maurice. He came to see me and told me that I had to cancel the show.

FRANK He did?

She nods.

JANEEN And what did you say?

FRANK She told him to look out her window.

JOHANNE laughs.

JANEEN What?

FRANK It's the new bureaucratic way of handling difficult people.

JOHANNE Maurice is a very good artist.

JANEEN Is he getting the studio?

JOHANNE We'll find out next week.

FRANK You don't know?

JOHANNE We'll all know next week.

JANEEN I like this series of "wearin'-gear and not-wearin'-gear" shots.

JOHANNE For me what's interesting is how they even stand differently depending on what they have on.

JANEEN It's almost as if the clothes are wearing them.

FRANK Some were quite surprised themselves.

JOHANNE And this. Maybe it's the places where I go to eat, but I have never seen a Black female chef. *Jamais.* I hope she gets to create the dish that she seems to be dreaming of. And him in this picture. *Comment on appele ça – cette espèce de pantalon en cuir?*

FRANK Chaps.

JOHANNE Chaps. Even for me that's sexy.

FRANK This married couple went to so much effort to get this shot perfect; the period outfits, the background, everything, except she's holding the pitchfork. And it works. I like it.

JOHANNE *Gothique noir. Ça marche pour moi aussi.*

JANEEN Now this is the one that sold me. He's what, seventy years old?

FRANK Seventy-two.

JOHANNE Wearing full hockey equipment.

FRANK For the first time in his life.

JANEEN It must be an amazing sensation to be laughing so fully and crying so deeply at the same time.

JOHANNE *Ah, celle-ci, elle est mignonne.*

FRANK My daughter, Anya. Isn't she cute in that horned helmet. Can I tell you something? Up until that moment I never knew that she had an interest in opera. All along I thought I knew everything about her. She said she was too embarrassed to tell anyone because they would laugh at her. I'm her father. I would never laugh at her.

JANEEN I'm sure she knows that.

FRANK She damn well better.

JOHANNE *Quelle Valkyrie.* If your daughter is interested she could speak with my partner who is always listening to Jessye Norman, Grace Bumbry, and Measha Brueggergosman.

FRANK Should I know these people?

JANEEN Maybe.

Suddenly we hear MAURICE, outside the gallery, yelling:

MAURICE Don't go in there. The rest of you inside, come out. Don't encourage that kind of thing. He's not an artist. He's a fraud. You've been had. Anybody could do what he's done. Leave now. "This is us/Ça c'est nous?" What's that all about? The whole thing's meaningless and empty and that's why I'm gonna shut it down.

Immediately the lights come up on the Funny Bones Comedy Club. However, there's no one on stage. A few moments later a figure from offstage hesitantly wanders towards the light. It's SHERMAN. He fumbles with the microphone, and, unaccustomed to the light's glare, he shields his eyes.

SHERMAN Good evening. The regularly scheduled comedian will not be here tonight. He is experiencing severe physical pain, the source of which doctors are unable to locate. His condition has not responded to medication and he is being held overnight for observation. In his absence he has requested that music by Abba be played. I thank you for your understanding. Goodnight.

He exits. Lights down.

16th FRAME — BOWLED OVER

Lights up. Sunday night. PINTO is lying in a hospital bed. FRANK enters.

FRANK Oh my God. Are you okay? I came as soon as I heard.

PINTO It's okay. I'm okay. They're just keeping me for observation. I'll be out tomorrow.

FRANK What happened?

PINTO Nothing. I mean nothing specific or obvious. After Sherman and I finished bowling the other night I started to feel tingling sensations in my arm and legs. Then this morning I could barely move.

FRANK This is amazing. What are the doctors saying?

PINTO That they've never seen anything like it before.

FRANK Are you in pain?

PINTO No. I just feel helpless. This has been a humbling experience. I didn't need to be humbled any further.

FRANK It's partly my fault. If I hadn't pushed you to go, none of this would have happened. I feel responsible. I've been saying that a lot lately.

PINTO No, no, you were right and I'm glad I listened, but I'm never going bowling again.

FRANK Oh I almost forgot. I brought you something. Well, it's from Dorothy. Some of her sweet potato dish. She made me promise you'd eat some.

PINTO That was very nice of her, but even if I wanted to I can't even feed myself.

FRANK I can.

PINTO I know you can feed yourself, don't rub—

FRANK No. I meant I can feed you.

PINTO What? No, no that won't be necessary.

FRANK I know, but I'd like to.

PINTO Frank, you know my eating problem. Do you think letting someone feed me—

FRANK Just a couple of mouthfuls. I'd like to. Please. I promised Dorothy.

PINTO No way.

FRANK Just try.

PINTO It's as though you don't believe me, I can't—

FRANK There are a lot of things that I've said I couldn't do, but I did them in spite of myself. Just try. Push yourself a little. That's all I'm asking.

PINTO And that's a lot.

FRANK It's really good. C'mon. Please.

PINTO Frank, you're not hearing me. Thank Dorothy for me, but I'll eat it some other time. When I'm alone. Maybe one day I'll have a meal with you, but not now. And definitely not here.

FRANK I'd like that.

FRANK puts the food away.

I told Dorothy about the picture. I told her how I had Germaine removed. She slapped me, then cried. I cried too. We then made incredible love, like we haven't in a long time.

PINTO What's going to happen now?

FRANK I don't know. I'm going to go looking for him.

PINTO And when you find him, remember your weak spot.

FRANK I'll try.

PINTO Hey, I've written some new material. Wanna hear it?

FRANK Sure.

PINTO Guy walks into a bar and says to the bartender, "I'd like a Scotch, single malt, and some soda on the side." Bartender says, "Normally that's $8.50, but because you're Black it'll cost you $17." The guy says, "I'm not Black, I'm God's Colour." Bartender says, "Oh, why didn't you say so. In that case, the drink's free."

FRANK reaches for the food. Lights out.

It's a joke, Frank, it's a joke.

End.

photo by Shelley Tepperman

Born in St. Michael, Barbados in 1951, Vadney S. Haynes has lived in Montreal for more than 50 years. He divides his time between teaching Psychology at Champlain Regional College and his private Psychotherapy practice. Academic interests saw him pursue a Bachelor's degree in Applied Social Science at Concordia University, a Masters degree in Educational Psychology and Counselling at McGill University and Doctoral studies in Psychology at the Université de Montréal.

At various times Vadney S. Haynes has been a producer, broadcaster and music programmer for radio stations in Montreal, and he had a brief stint as a freelance music critic for the *Montreal Gazette*. His passion for music is matched by his love for film and CFL football. *Blacks Don't Bowl* is his first produced play.